Grateful
Hearts
Give
Thanks

Bob & Emilie Barnes

HARVEST HOUSE PUBLISHERS
Eugene, Oregon

This book is dedicated to all the families throughout the world who gather together to thank the Lord for His abundance.

By carrying on this tradition of thanksgiving, we show our children and others that we worship a God who is the Creator of all things. We as humble people fold our hands or join them together in a united circle to express our utmost appreciation to Him.

We thank God that you are making a difference in your home, your neighborhood, your community, your state, your nation, and your world. May you be richly blessed as you steadfastly honor God by giving your thanks unto Him.

Grateful Hearts Give Thanks
Text Copyright © 2000 Harvest House Publishers
Eugene, Oregon 97402

Library of Congress Cataloging-in-Publication Data
Barnes, Bob, 1933-
    Grateful hearts give thanks / Bob and Emilie Barnes
        p. cm.
    ISBN 0-7369-0129-9
    1. Prayers. 2. Gratitude–Religious aspects–Christianity. I. Barnes, Emilie.

BV245 .B326 2000
242'.8–dc21   00-028129

Design and production by Koechel Peterson and Associates, Minneapolis, Minnesota

The authors and Harvest House Publishers have made every effort to trace the ownership of all poems and quotes. In the event of a question arising from the use of a poem or quote, we regret any error made and will be pleased to make the necessary correction in future editions of this book.

Unless otherwise indicated, Scripture quotations are taken from the Holy Bible, New International Version®, Copyright © 1973, 1978, 1984 by the International Bible Society. Used by permission of Zondervan Publishing House. Scripture quotations marked NASB are from the New American Standard Bible, © 1960, 1962, 1963, 1968, 1971, 1972, 1973, 1975, 1977 by The Lockman Foundation. Used by permission.

00 01 02 03 04 05 06 07 08 09 / IM / 10 9 8 7 6 5 4 3 2 1

Contents

"Thank You, God"

I will praise God's name in song and glorify him with thanksgiving.

PSALM 69:30

One of the great joys in life is to give thanks to God for all abundance of life. We can do it in prayers, in songs, in graces, and in blessings. We can do it for all occasions—births, dedications, housewarmings, graduations, weddings, anniversaries, and many more. Life gives us a multitude of opportunities to say, "Thank You, Lord." The tradition of saying blessings and graces is a wholesome and biblical way of echoing our gratitude back to God.

It is important to gather our families and friends together for prayer at life's special times—times of celebration, times of achievement, times of change, times of growth, times of transition. In addition, a simple grace at mealtime and a blessing before bedtime are time-honored traditions and sources of spiritual connection for many believers.

Whether you are gifted in praying aloud or are fairly new to this sacred art, you will find that this book will bring inspiration to your meals and special gatherings.

Graces bring us closer together, keep us in touch with God, and help us to remember our fellow men and women in need.

Offering thanks does not make the food into something it wasn't, but it does make the partakers into something they may not have previously been—thankful. These prayers for all ages help people to discover great truths and to speak in a language of gratitude. Regular worship leads people to thankfulness and lifts even the most discouraged soul to a higher level of praise.

This book is a compilation of poems, prayers, invocations, songs, and salutations that have been gathered from many sources—friends, family members, pastors, and famous people. Some sources are known, some are anonymous. Every effort has been taken to give proper credit to the original author.

Leave this book on your dining room table as a daily reminder to read from it. The family will soon become so attached to the readings that they will request the prayers if someone forgets. After awhile you might even ask someone at the table if they would like to give their very own blessing.

May these graces, blessings, and thanksgivings give you the inspiration to say, "Thank You, God, for all You have given us."

—Bob and Emilie

Thanksgiving

The Lord's Prayer

Our Father who art in heaven,

Hallowed be Thy name.

Thy kingdom come.

Thy will be done,

On earth as it is in heaven.

Give us this day our daily bread.

And forgive us our debts, as we also have forgiven our debtors.

And do not lead us into temptation, but deliver us from evil.

For Thine is the kingdom, and the power, and the glory, forever.

Amen.

Matthew 6:9-13 NASB

O God, who givest us not only the day for labor and the night for rest, but also the peace of this blessed day; grant, we beseech Thee, that its quiet may be profitable to us in heavenly things, and refresh and strengthen us to finish the work which Thou hast given us to do; through Jesus Christ our Lord. Amen.

JAMES MARTINEAU

Grant us grace, Almighty Father, so to pray as to deserve to be heard.

Jane Austen

We thank Thee for the good things of this life, for food and raiment and shelter; for work to do and zest in the doing of it. We thank Thee for the perpetual touch of the divine in life, for the image of Thyself in the soul of man; for the vigor of youth, the wisdom of age, and for all the lessons of experience; the steps by which we climb to higher things; for the courage of the brave, the indignation of the righteous, the kindness of the thoughtful, and all that makes us men and keeps us Godlike.

HUBERT SIMPSON

Because your love is better than life, my lips will glorify you.

PSALM 63:3

Speak, Lord, for Thy servant heareth. Grant us ears to hear, eyes to see, wills to obey, hearts to love; then declare what Thou wilt, reveal what Thou wilt, command what Thou wilt, demand what Thou wilt—Amen.

CHRISTINA ROSSETTI

May the Lord, mighty God, bless
    and keep you forever.
Grant you peace, perfect peace, courage
    in every endeavor.
Lift up your eyes and see His face,
    and His grace forever.
May the Lord, mighty God, bless
    and keep you forever.

TRADITIONAL

Eternal Father of my soul, let my first
thought today be of Thee, let my first
impulse be to worship Thee, let my first
speech be Thy name, let my first action be
to kneel before Thee in prayer.

JOHN BAILLIE

To be thankful for what I have received, and for what my Lord has prepared, is the surest way to receive more. ANDREW MURRAY

Prayer of St. Francis

Lord, make me an instrument of Your peace; where there is hatred, let me sow love;

where there is injury, pardon; where there is doubt, faith; where there is despair, hope;

where there is darkness, light; where there is sadness, joy.

O Divine Master, grant that I may not so much seek to be consoled as to console; to be

understood as to understand; to be loved as to love; for it is in giving that we receive,

it is in pardoning that we are pardoned, and it is in dying that we are born to eternal life.

St. Francis of Assisi

8

May the wisdom of God instruct me,
the eye of God watch over me,
the ear of God hear me,
the word of God give me sweet talk,
the hand of God defend me,
the way of God guide me.

Christ be with me.
Christ before me.
Christ in me.
Christ under me.
Christ over me.
Christ on my right hand.
Christ on my left hand.
Christ on this side.
Christ on that side.
Christ in the head of everyone to whom I speak.
Christ in the mouth of every person who speaks to me.
Christ in the eye of every person who looks upon me.
Christ in the ear of everyone who hears me...
Amen.

ST. PATRICK

Almighty God, Father of all mercies,

we Your unworthy servants give You

humble thanks for all Your goodness and

loving-kindness to us and to all men.

We bless You for our creation, preservation,

and all the blessings of this life;

but above all for Your incomparable love in the redemption

of the world by our Lord Jesus Christ;

for the means of grace, and for the hope of glory.

Our Father, let the spirit of gratitude

so prevail in our hearts that we may manifest

Thy spirit in our lives. Amen.

W.B. Slack

Teach us, good Lord, to serve Thee as Thou deservest; to give and not to count the cost; to fight and not to head the wounds; to toil and not to seek for rest; to labor and not to ask for any reward, save that of knowing that we do Thy will; through Jesus Christ our Lord. Amen.

IGNATIUS OF LOYOLA

And we pray, give us such awareness of Your mercies, that with truly thankful hearts we may make known Your praise, not only with our lips, but in our lives, by giving up ourselves to Your service, and by walking before You in holiness and righteousness all our days; through Jesus Christ our Lord, to whom, with You and the Holy Spirit, be all honor and glory throughout the ages. Amen.

STANDARD BOOK OF COMMON PRAYER

Give thanks to the Lord,
for he is good;
his love endures forever.

1 CHRONICLES 16:34

I will praise God's name in song and glorify him with thanksgiving. PSALM 69:30

Lord, we thank You for Your grace,
our needs are met here in this place.
We trust You in Your sovereign way,
to lead us closer day by day. Amen.

Truro Heights

Lord, we give Thee but Thine own,
  Whate'er the gift may be:
All that we have is Thine alone,
  A trust, O Lord, from Thee.

May we Thy bounties thus
  As stewards true receive,
And gladly, as Thou blessest us,
  To Thee our first-fruits give.

To comfort and to bless,
  To find a balm for woe,
To tend the lone and fatherless,
  Is angels' work below.

The captive to release,
  To God the lost to bring,
To teach the way of life and peace,
  It is a Christ-like thing.

And we believe Thy word,
  Though dim our faith may be,
Whate'er for Thine we do, O Lord,
  We do it unto Thee.

William Walsham How

12

We thank the Lord for food and drink,
for appetite and power to think,
for loved ones dear, for home and friends,
for everything the good Lord sends.

KIM LUDIKER

We thank Thee, O God, for every blessing
of soul and body, and do Thou add this, O
Lord, to Thy other mercies, that we may
praise Thee not with our lips only, but with
our lives, always looking to Thee as the
Author and Giver of all good things.

BISHOP BROOKE FOSS WESTCOTT

Enter his gates with thanksgiving and his courts with praise;

give thanks to him and praise his name. PSALM 100:4

Dear God, I gratefully bow my head
To thank You for this daily bread;
And may there be a goodly share
On every table everywhere. Amen.

DIXIE WILLSON

Be present at our table, Lord,
Be here and everywhere adored.
The creatures bless, and grant that we
May feast in paradise with Thee. Amen.

JOHN WESLEY

I will be glad and rejoice in you; I will sing praise to your name, O Most High. PSALM 9:2

*I will give thanks to the Lord
because of his righteousness
and will sing praise to the name
of the Lord Most High.*

Psalm 7:17

Gratitude for Each Day

Thou that hast given so much to me,

Give one thing more,—a grateful heart;

Not thankful when it pleaseth me.

Gratefulness

As if Thy blessings had spare days,

But such a heart whose pulse may be

Thy praise.

George Herbert

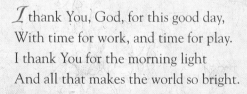

I thank You, God, for this good day,
With time for work, and time for play.
I thank You for the morning light
And all that makes the world so bright.

Help me to live this lovely day
In such a kind and friendly way.
You will be glad that I am here
To help You fill the world with cheer.

FRANCES McKINNON MORTON

All good things around us
Are sent from heaven above.
We thank the Lord,
O thank the Lord,
For all His love. Amen.

Matthias Claudius

I thank God and I praise Him

for the sunset that lifts my spirit,

the morning that lets my

soul take flight in search

of wildflowers, the songbirds that

waken my world. And I

thank God for His presence

in my life, for family and friends,

for joy and even for sorrows

that strengthen my life, for

the awareness that

God's love is the essence of

all happiness, the bond between

heaven and earth.

Neil C. Fitzgerald

Praise the Lord for sunshine,
Praise the Lord for rain,
Praise the Lord for pleasure,
Praise the Lord for pain,
Praise the Lord for lessons learned
Through every joy and sorrow,
Praise the Lord for days gone by,
And for each new tomorrow!

ALICE JOYCE DAVIDSON

We thank You, Lord, for Your steadfast love, and for Your wonderful works to the sons of men. You satisfy those who are thirsty and fill their hunger with good things. Amen.

BOB AND EMILIE BARNES

The sun is shining...thank You, Lord. I mean it is shining: the sky and everything is warm and smiling.

But it is not only that...my heart is smiling. I know that I am loved...and that I love too. Thank You, Lord, the sun is shining.

MICHAEL HOLLINGS AND ETTA GULLICK

Gracious God, smile on us in tender mercy. Help us to be humble and truly thankful for these and all other blessings. Amen. BOB AND EMILIE BARNES

I give thanks, O God,
for all You have so lovingly done for me!
For each need comes Your faithfulness.
During suffering comes Your compassion.
On every journey comes Your closeness.
My deepest praise sings out in a blended anthem with
believers all over the world—thanking You for the abundant
life found in Christ Jesus!

Charlotte Adelsperger

Mealtime Prayers

O Lord, who is the giver of all good things, fill our hearts with gratitude for the food and drink laid before us. And as we fill our bellies, may we be sober and frugal in our eating, taking only that which is necessary to refresh ourselves for Your service. Let the pleasure we take in the bread that nourishes our earthly bodies be as nothing to the joy we take in the spiritual bread of Your truth, which nourishes the soul.

John Calvin

Bless this meal, O God, we pray,
And bless us, too, throughout the day.
Keep us safe and close to You,
And kind in all we say and do. Amen.

THERESA MARY GRASS

As we now from Thy bounty eat,
keep us humble, kind, and sweet.
May we serve Thee, Lord, each day,
and feel Thy love, Dear Lord, we pray.

LUELLA FREAR

We who sit together here,
wish to thank You, Father Dear,
for Thy love and tender care,
folded round us everywhere. Amen.

LOIS KAUFMAN

Bless this home and all who love it, as we break bread in fellowship with Thee and one another. Amen.   ALAN R. CHALMERS

To God who gives us daily bread
    A thankful song we raise,
And pray that He who sends us food
    Will fill our hearts with praise. Amen.

Mary Rumsey

Blest are You, Lord, God of our fathers. Through Your goodness we enjoy the fruits of the earth and share the loving gifts of family and friendship. We ask Your blessing on our guests, our table, and our home. We offer thanks for the love with which this festive meal was prepared, and for the love and joy which brings us together to partake of it. In gratitude for Your continued care over us, make us mindful of the needs of others, that we may show our thanks in the manner of our living. May our hearts be filled with love and praise, as we pray to Your holy name. Amen.

Eileen Chaney

Blessed art Thou,
O Lord, our King,
Who feedest every
Living thing;

Who givest bread,
So that we may
Have strength to do
Our work each day.

Blessed art Thou
For Thou does give
Food to nourish
All that live.

ILO ORLEANS

Unto Him Who through breaking of bread brought us close to God, HENRY SYLVESTER NASH be all honor and glory now and evermore. Amen.

Father, we thank Thee for this
         wonderful day,
for all our blessings along life's way.
Guide us, protect us, and forgive all our sins,
and be ever present as this meal now begins.
         Amen.

EVELYN DIETZ

In all these bounties, dear Lord, help us to
see You behind them. To your greater glory
and to our good, in Christ's name. Amen.

BOB AND EMILIE BARNES

Our Father, We thank Thee for this food,
remembering those who are hungry. We thank
Thee for our health, remembering those who
are ill. We thank Thee for our homes,
remembering those who are homeless. We
thank Thee for our friends, remembering
those who are friendless. We thank Thee for
these blessings and ask Thee to bless those
without them. Amen.

EMMA STREENZ

Come, dear Lord,
    be our guest and
become our host.
         Be pleased to
bless this food and
us who dwell here.
Amen.

Bob and Emilie Barnes

O Thou, who kindly dost provide

For every creature's want!

We bless Thee, God of nature wide,

For all Thy goodness lent:

And, if it please Thee, heavenly Guide,

May never worse be sent;

But, whether granted or denied,

Lord, bless us with content! Amen.

Robert Burns

Bedtime Prayers

As the evening falls, dear Lord,
and while I seek Your face in
prayers, grant me the joy of
good friends, the creative power of
new interests, and the peace of a
quiet heart. As darkness comes grant
me light to judge the errors and the
wisdom of the day's work.
And grant me again the healing
touch of sleep. Amen.

Author Unknown

Praised be Thou, O Lord our God,
Father of all,
for giving us the sweet rest of the night.
In peace do I lay me down to sleep,
and may it be Thy will, O Lord,
that I awake in peace.
I am in the care of the Lord
when I sleep and when I wake.
In Thy help I trust, O Lord, Amen.

HYMAN E. GOLDIN

Lord of the springtime, Father of flower,
field and fruit, smile on us in these earnest
days when the work is heavy and the toil
wearisome; lift up our hearts, O God, to the
things worthwhile—sunshine and night, the
dripping rain, the song of the birds, books and
music, and the voices of our friends. Lift up
our hearts to these this night and grant us
Thy peace. Amen.

W.E.B. DuBois

Father, keep me safe tonight. Bless Thy child again. Help me always do the right.
In Christ's name, Amen. FREDERICK HILL MESERVE

I thank Thee, Father, for the way
Thy hand has guided me today.
I woke at morning's dawn afraid
to face my problems so I prayed.
And one by one each need was met,
for Thou hast never failed me yet.
Dear God, henceforth my prayer shall be
for strong, abiding faith in Thee.
Amen.

VIRGINIA SCOTT MAROUS

Now the day is over,
Night is drawing nigh,
Shadows of the evening
Steal across the sky;

Jesus, give the weary
Calm and sweet repose;
With Thy tender blessing
May our eyelids close.

Grant to little children
Visions bright of Thee;
Guard the sailors tossing
On the deep, blue sea.

Through the long night watches,
May Thine angels spread
Their white wings above me,
Watching round my bed.

When the morning wakens
Then may I arise
Pure, and fresh, and sinles
In Thy holy eyes. Amen.

Sabine Baring-Gould

26

Jesus, tender Shepherd, hear me;
Bless Thy little lamb tonight;
Through the darkness be Thou near me,
Keep me safe till morning light.

All this day Thy hand has led me,
And I thank Thee for Thy care;
Thou has warmed me, clothed and fed me;
Listen to my evening prayer!

Let my sins be all forgiven;
Bless the friends I love so well:
Take us all at last to heaven,
Happy there with Thee to dwell.

MARY DUNCAN

Lord, should we oft forget to sing
A thankful evening song of praise,
This duty they to mind might bring
Who chirp among the bushy sprays.
For to their perches they retire,
When first the twilight waxeth dim,
And every night that sweet-voiced choir
Shuts up the daylight with a hymn.

Ten thousand-fold more cause have we
To close each day with praiseful voice,
To offer thankful hearts to Thee,
And in Thy mercies to rejoice.
Therefore for all Thy mercies past,
For those this evening doth afford,
And which for times to come Thou hast,
We give Thee hearty thanks, O Lord!

GEORGE WITHER

EVENSONG

The embers of the day are red
      Beyond the murky hill.
   The kitchen smokes; the bed
In the darkling house is spread:
      The great sky darkens overhead,
   And the great woods are shrill.
   So far have I been led,
            Lord, by Thy will:
So far I have followed, Lord, and I wondered still.
   The breeze from the embalmed land
Blows sudden towards the shore,
And claps my cottage door.
   I hear the signal, Lord—I understand.
            The night at Thy command
Comes. I will eat and sleep
      and will not question more.

Robert Louis Stevenson

Prayers for Others

The blessings of God rest upon all those who have been kind to us, have cared for us, have worked for us, have served us, have shared our bread at this table. Our merciful God, reward all of them in Your own way, for Yours is the glory and the honor forever.

St. Cyril of Alexandria

Give us grateful hearts,
    our Father,
    for all Thy mercies,
        and make us mindful
    of the needs of others.

The Book of Common Prayer

Most gracious God, we beseech Thee for all who are near and dear to us; for little children, that they may be kept in their innocence; for aged folk, that they may have clear shining at eventide; for men busy with the affairs of life, and women burdened with household cares, that the peace of God may fill their hearts and minds; and for dear friends who are far away, that thou wouldst have them in Thy safe keeping and spare us to meet again in Thy peace and joy.

JOHN WATSON

The Lord bless you and keep you;
the Lord make his face to shine upon you
    and be gracious to you;
the Lord turn his face toward you
    and give you peace.

THE AARONIC BLESSING, NUMBERS 6:24-26

Dear Lord, the abundance of our table declares Your goodness. Forbid that we should hide ourselves from those in need, whether materially or spiritually. Amen.

BOB AND EMILIE BARNES

As You have blessed me, dear Lord, so make me a blessing to someone this day Through my Savior, Jesus Christ. Amen. BOB AND EMILIE BARNES

O blessed Lord, who hast commanded us to love one another, grant us grace that having received Thine undeserved bounty, we may love everyone in Thee and for Thee. We implore Thy clemency for all; but especially for the friends whom Thy love has given to us. Love Thou them, O Thou fountain of love, and make them to love Thee with all their heart, that they may will, and speak, and do those things only which are pleasing to Thee.

ST. ANSELM

Family Prayers

Father,

    Grant unto us true family love,

  That we may belong more entirely to those whom Thou hast given us,

Understanding each other, day by day, more instinctively,

    Forbearing each other, day by day, more patiently,

  Growing, day by day, more closely into oneness with each other.

     Father,

       Thou too art love:

    Thou knowest the depth of pain and the height of glory

      Which abide continually in love:

        Make us perfect in love for these our dear ones,

    As knowing that without them we can never be made perfect in Thee.

Father,

    Bring to full fruit in us Thine own nature,

  That nature of humble redemptive devotion,

    Which, out of two responsive souls,

      Can create a new heaven and a new earth,

  One eternal glory of divine self-sharing.

Anonymous

Our Heavenly Father, we thank You for this food, the roof above us and for this family. Help us remember that a family is for growing up in, for going away from, and for coming back to. It is for loving concern, for helping each other through happy times and sad. With Your blessing, this family will always be together in our hearts and in our memories, giving each of us the strength to live our own lives and to be our own persons. Amen.

VIRGINIA BACKUS

Lord, behold our family here assembled.
We thank You for this place in which we dwell,
for the love that unites us,
for the peace accorded us this day,
for the hope with which we expect the morrow;
for the health, the work, the food,
    the bright skies
that make our lives delightful;
for our friends in all parts of the earth. Amen.

ROBERT LOUIS STEVENSON

Heavenly Father, here we gather holding hands with those we love. Thank You for the food before us and all the blessings from above. Amen. BERNIE SLATTERY

Children's Prayers

Dear God, I thank You for my parents…for all their wise and careful instruction. When my feet were small, they lovingly set them upon the right paths. I thank them for all the times they comforted me when I was hurt or afraid and listened to how I felt. As I grew, they showed me to see beauty when I was broken, brought me gladness when I was sad, praised and encouraged me when all seemed lost. Thanks for all their secret prayers for me. They've been my best friends here on earth and if God hadn't chosen them to be my parents…I would have picked them anyway. Amen.

Author Unknown

Dear God, again I bow my head,
And thank Thee for my daily bread.
I thank Thee, God, again today
That I am well, that I can play.
Thank Thee for friends so good to me;
Help me a good, kind friend to be. Amen.

NORMAN S. SCHLICHTER

Bless our food and drink, Dear Lord,
and bless our little friends, too.
Help us day by day to show
our love and thanks to You. Amen.

RACHEL ADAMS

May all that we do and all that we say,
help to brighten someone's day.
And may this meal give strength today,
to do Your will at work and play.

SHARON HOLCOMB

Father God,
thanks for Mother's love and Father's care,
for food to eat and clothes to wear;
for homes and friends and answered prayer,
we thank You, God. Amen.

RYAN BURNETT

We thank Thee, Lord, for happy hearts, for rain and sunny weather.
We thank Thee, Lord, for this our food, and that we are together. Amen.

EMILIE FENDALL JOHNSON

Ah, dearest Jesus, holy Child,
Make Thee a bed, soft, undefiled,
Within my heart, that it may be
A quiet chamber kept for Thee.

Martin Luther

Dear Father, hear and bless
Thy beasts and singing birds,
And guard with tenderness
Small things that have no words.

AUTHOR UNKNOWN

Thank You for the world so sweet, thank You for the food we eat, Thank You for the birds that sing

Now before I run to play,

Let me not forget to pray

To God who kept me through the night

And waked me with the morning light.

Help me, Lord, to love Thee more

Than I ever loved before,

In my works and in my play,

Be Thou with me through the day. Amen.

Author Unknown

He prayeth well, who loveth well
　　Both man and bird and beast.
He prayeth best, who loveth best
　　All things both great and small;
For the dear God who loveth us,
　　He made and loveth all.

SAMUEL TAYLOR COLERIDGE

Thank You, God, for everything.   MRS. E. R. LEATHAM

Parents' Prayers

O God, our heavenly Father, have mercy
upon our children. We humbly pray for them
and commend them to your gracious
protection. Be their guide and guardian in all
their endeavors. Lead them in the path of
Your truth and draw them near to You, that
they may lead a godly and righteous life in
Your love and fear, doing Your will in all
matters. Direct them in the way of salvation,
through Your Son, Jesus Christ. Amen.

Adapted from a traditional Orthodox prayer

*L*ord, bless my children and their children to have a life that is pleasing in Your sight. May they seek You first, Lord, so they can receive the blessings You have waiting for them. Keep them safe from harm. Give them wisdom to make the right decisions. I love You, Lord, and trust Your Word. Thank You for Your grace. Amen.

EARTHA TAYLOR

*W*e give thanks for our children. May we continue to be blessed by their simple wonder so that we might not take for granted one single moment of this miracle to which we've been born. Amen.

STEVE MYRVANG

PRAYERS OF THANKS FOR
God's Creation

I thank You, my Creator and Lord, that You have given me these joys in Your creation, this ecstasy over the works of Your hands. I have made known the glory of your works to men as far as my finite spirit was able to comprehend your infinity. If I have said anything wholly unworthy of You, or have aspired after my own glory, graciously forgive me. Amen.

Johannes Kepler

God of the wide distances of the world, lift Thou my eyes to far horizons. Grant me to see the long course of history out of which my single self and this vast world have come. Bring that which is far away close, because I see and understand it. Amen.

BOB AND EMILIE BARNES

You crown the year with your bounty, and your carts overflow with abundance. The grasslands of the desert overflow; the hills are clothed with gladness. The meadows are covered with flocks and the valleys are mantled with grain; they shout for joy and sing.

PSALM 65:12,13

We give You everlasting thanks, O God, For the marvels of Your great creation. As the flowers blossom and bloom around us We lift our hearts in joy and celebration. Amen.

JOYCE BLAKNEY DUERR

We thank Thee, God, as we watch the distant hills suddenly emerge above the filmy, white mist and gently touch heaven— awakening the sun for another day.

JOAN STEPHEN

All things bright and beautiful,
All creatures great and small,
All things wise and wonderful:
The Lord God made them all. Amen.

C.F. Alexander

Father God, to see a world in a grain of sand and a heaven in a wildflower, WILLIAM BLAKE
Hold infinity in the palm of your hand and eternity in an hour.

Special Gatherings and Occasions

Here is to loving, to romance, to us.

May we travel together through time.

We alone count as none, but together we're one,

For our partnership puts love to rhyme.

Irish Blessing

Anniversaries

Birthdays

We come together to celebrate the birthday of [name]. We give thanks to God for the life and hope that is within [name], whose birth we celebrate in the name of the Father, and of the Son, and of the Holy Spirit. Amen.

BOB AND EMILIE BARNES

God grant you many and happy years,
Till, when the last has crowned you,
The dawn of endless days appears,
And heaven is shining round you!

OLIVER WENDELL HOLMES

Father God, as we meet to celebrate [name's] birthday, we want to pause and thank You for giving him/her this added year of life on this earth. May he/she continue in Your richest blessing, good health. May this next year be prosperous and beneficial to Your glory. Amen.

BOB AND EMILIE BARNES

To wish you joy on your birthday
And all the whole year through,
For all the best that life can hold
Is none too good for you.

BOB AND EMILIE BARNES

Many happy returns of the day of your birth: Many blessings to brighten your pathway on earth; ROBERT H. LORD

O Jesus, shed Thy tender love

Upon me, please, today.

On this my birthday give me grace

My special prayer to say.

Few are my candles, few my years;

So let my promise be

That all the years that I may live

I'll love and worship Thee.

Author Unknown

Birthdays

I ask and wish not to appear
More beauteous, rich or gay:
Lord, make me wiser every year,
And better every day.

Charles Lamb

Father God, as we dedicate this new

home to You, we want You to be at

the center of all our activities. May

each room be protected for its intent.

We know that You are the provider

of all good gifts and this home is

certainly from You. May this house

become a home for its occupants. May

it reflect the security, safety, warmth,

and hospitality of a godly home. May

Jesus be glorified in all that is said and

done within these walls. Amen.

Bob and Emilie Barnes

House Blessings

May blessings be upon your
   house,
Your roof and hearth and walls;
May there be lights to
      welcome you
When evening's shadow falls—
The love that like a guiding star
Still signals when you roam;
A book, a friend—these be
      the things
That make a house a home.

MYRTLE REED

I pray Heaven to bestow the best
blessings on this house and all that
shall hereafter inhabit it. May
none but honest and wise men
rule under this roof.

JOHN ADAMS

God of mercy,
God of grace,
Be pleased to bless
This dwelling place.
May peace and kindly deed
Be found;
May gratitude and love
Abound.

NORMA WOODBRIDGE

House Blessings

Bless this house, Lord, and those who live here,
   in the name of the Father, and of the Son,
   and of the Holy Spirit. We pray that this home
      might be a reflection of the grace-filled home,
blessed by Christ Himself, as we ask Your blessing.
We pray that Your Spirit may rest in the hearts of this family
   and in this home, as we ask Your blessing. Amen.

Bob and Emilie Barnes

Almighty and ever-blessed God, whose presence is the happiness of every condition, and whose favor sweetens every relation; we beseech Thee to be present and favorable unto these Thy servants, that they may be truly joined in the honorable estate of marriage; as Thou hast brought them together by Thy providence, sanctify them by Thy Spirit, giving them a new frame of heart for their new estate; and grant unto them, now in the hour of their affiance and throughout their wedded life, Thy heavenly guidance; through our Lord Jesus Christ. Amen.

The Book of Common Worship

Weddings

Father God, as we gather for the wedding of
[name] and [name], we bring them to You as a couple
who have put their faith in Your leadership
for their lives. May they always look to You for direction and
guidance. May they always be committed to the vows
that they have made to You this day. We who are
gathered together offer our prayers and encouragement
to help them along the way of becoming one in spirit.
Bless their lives abundantly. Amen.

BOB AND EMILIE BARNES

Graduation

Father God, [name] has attained a level of academic standard for which we are proud. We thank You for giving him/her a sound mind, a discipline for study, a proficiency for adaptability, and a desire to fulfill an academic goal for life. May the knowledge gained become wisdom with the maturity of time, and may it be but a stepping stone to the next challenge in life. May [name] always continue to learn and realize that life is a process of growth. May Your blessing be abundantly given as he/she lives a life worthy of Your calling. In Jesus' name we pray. Amen.

BOB AND EMILIE BARNES

New Baby

Father God, what a joy to welcome [name] into our lives. As we look at the miracle of birth and all that it entails, we marvel at Your majesty. This birth is another reminder that You are the Creator and we are Your creatures. May You bless this child with good health, good parents, a good family, grandparents who will come alongside the parents to mentor and offer prayer support along the way. We humbly acknowledge that You are the giver of all life. May we collectively show good stewardship in raising this child. Amen.

Bob and Emilie Barnes

Father God, as spring shows its head from the cold of the frozen snow, we thank You for all the seeds to be sown, the glittering of the leaves on the fruit trees, the sweet smell of the flowers that will bloom, and the birth of newborns. This season vividly reinforces the greatness of You the Creator. Amen.

BOB AND EMILIE BARNES

Father God, I already feel the added warmth of the sun as You usher in summer. The sunshine warms the ground so we can have abundance in the fields. This season provides us with all the food that we need to live throughout the rest of the year. Thank You, Lord. Amen.

BOB AND EMILIE BARNES

Seasons of the Year

For scents that herald springtime
For lilac-haunted nooks
For violet's purple fragrance
    And merry, trickling brooks—
For little things that give soul wings—
    I thank Thee. Amen.

Monica Miller

In wintertime when limbs are bare I find
things of which I was not aware;
The nest of birds and squirrels and bees,
and mistletoe clinging to the trees.
But when a blanket of snow is supplied
the world seems somehow purified.
Oh how close to Heaven can I be with all
this beauty surrounding me! Amen.

MARY A. SUMMERLINE

Father God, the leaves are turning yellow,
orange, and red to usher in the majestic
colors of fall. This is a time to bless
You for giving us the abundance of
our crops. During this season we get to
rest our bodies and equipment from the
toils of summer. I want to reflect back
and thank You for all your abundance.
We are thankful people.

BOB AND EMILIE BARNES

Father God, the streets and fields are white with Your kisses of snow.

As we usher in winter we want to reflect back on Your holiness and purity.

As white colors our wayside we want to enter into a new covenant

with You that our lives will reflect Your purity. You have been a great God this year.

Thank You for Your faithfulness to us as a people. Amen.

Bob and Emilie Barnes

Holiday Prayers

Father God, as we start this new year

we pledge a thankful heart for all abundance You have given us.

We thank You for the previous year,

and we ask for continued favor for this new year.

Give us good health, good family times,

and general goodness of Your mercies. May You receive

all the glory in Jesus' name. Amen.

Bob and Emilie Barnes

O Thou who art from everlasting to everlasting, without beginning or end of days; replenish us with heavenly grace, at the beginning of this year, that we may be enabled to accept all its duties, to perform all its labors, to welcome all its mercies, to meet all its trials, and to advance through all it holds in store for us, with cheerful courage and a constant mind. O Lord, suffer us not to be separated from Thee, either by joy or sorrow, or by any sin or weakness of our own; but have compassion upon us, and forgive us, and keep us in the strong confidence of Thine eternal love in Jesus Christ; that as Thou hast called us to immortality through Him, so we may pass the residue of our years in the power of an endless life; and to Thy name shall be all the praise. Amen.

THE BOOK OF COMMON WORSHIP

Before the morning star begotten,
and Lord from everlasting,
our Savior is made manifest
unto the world today.

Epiphany, Office of Lauds, Western Rite

*A*lmighty God, *who at the baptism of thy blessed Son Jesus Christ in the river Jordan didst manifest His glorious Godhead; Grant, we beseech Thee, that the brightness of His presence may shine in our hearts, and His glory be set forth in our lives; through the same Jesus Christ our Lord.*

EPIPHANY, THE SCOTTISH PRAYER BOOK

O Lord God of our fathers, who in Thy goodness hast led this people hitherto by wondrous ways; who makest the nations to praise Thee, and knittest them together in the bonds of peace; we beseech Thee to pour thine abundant blessing on this nation over which Thou hast called Thy servant our President. Grant that all, of whatever race or color, or tongue, may, in prosperity and peace, be united in the bond of brotherhood, and in the one fellowship of the faith, so that we may be found a people acceptable unto Thee; through Jesus Christ our Lord. Amen.

ACTS OF DEVOTION

*F*ather God, as we come to You today to honor all the presidents who have made our country great, we give You honor for instilling goodness in these great men. We thank You for the vision they had, the sacrifices they made, and the dedication they had to make us a nation of freedom. May we never take for granted all they have done for our country. Amen.

BOB AND EMILIE BARNES

President's Day

O Lord, our Heavenly Father, the high and mighty Ruler of the universe, who dost from Thy throne behold all the dwellers upon earth; most heartily we beseech Thee with Thy favor to behold and bless Thy servant, the President of these United States, and all who make or execute our laws; and so replenish them with the graces of Thy Holy Spirit that they may always incline to Thy will, and walk in Thy way. Endow them plenteously with heavenly gifts; grant them health and prosperity long to live; and finally, after this life, to attain everlasting joy and felicity; through Jesus Christ our Lord. Amen.

The Book of Common Prayer

Almighty and everlasting God,
 who hatest nothing that Thou hast made,
 and dost forgive the sins of all them that are penitent;
  create and make in us new and contrite hearts,
 that we, worthily lamenting our sins,
may obtain of Thee, the God of all mercy,
  perfect remission and forgiveness;
 through Jesus Christ our Lord. Amen.

THE BOOK OF COMMON PRAYER

Ash Wednesday

Father God, we come to You this day to ask for forgiveness of our sins. We repent and ask for Your mercies. We ask that You give us added strength that we might not repeat these sins against You. May our lives reflect the grace that You extend to us. Amen.

Bob and Emilie Barnes

Father God, as we enter this week of Easter we remember the sacrifice You made to make us whole. We thank You for sending Your Son, Jesus, to be crucified on the cross for our sins. May we too lay down the palm fronds of our life that we might celebrate with You this precious gift of salvation. Amen.

Bob and Emilie Barnes

Our Father, as on this day we keep the special memory of our Redeemer's entry into the city, so grant, O Lord, that now and ever He may triumph in our hearts. Let the King of grace and glory enter in, and let us lay ourselves and all we are in full and joyful homage before Him; through the same Jesus Christ our Lord. Amen.

PRAYERS FOR THE CHRISTIAN YEAR

Almighty and everlasting God, who, of Thy tender love towards mankind, hast sent Thy Son, our Savior Jesus Christ, to take upon Him our flesh, and to suffer death upon the cross, that all mankind should follow the example of His great humility; mercifully grant that we may both follow the example of His patience, and also be made partners of His resurrection; through the same Jesus Christ our Lord. Amen.

THE BOOK OF COMMON PRAYER

Good Friday

Father God, as we come together to celebrate
this day of our Lord's crucifixion on the cross
at Calvary Mount, we humbly pray that
You will accept our thanks of appreciation
for the ultimate sacrifice of one man giving His life
for another. We ask You to bless the events
and food of this day. Amen.

Bob and Emilie Barnes

Father God, as we witness the sun coming in view,

we thank You for this new day.

Easter is a day of celebration for Your Son's victory over death.

May we, as believers, take this new day and live it to Your glory.

We are so thankful for what You did on the cross for us. Amen.

Bob and Emilie Barnes

Easter

We have seen the resurrection of Christ; let us worship the holy Lord Jesus, who alone is without sin. We praise and glorify Your holy resurrection. For You are our God; we know no other, save for You. Upon Your name we call. Come, all faithful ones, let us adore the holy resurrection of Christ, for through the Cross, joy has come to all the world. Ever blessing the Lord, we sing praises of His resurrection. He endured the cross on our behalf and has destroyed death by death. Amen.

SUNDAY VIGIL, ORTHODOX CHURCH

O Thou who makest the stars, and turnest the shadow of death into the morning; on this day of days we meet to render Thee, our Lord and King, the tribute of our praise; for the resurrection of the spring-time, for the everlasting hopes that rise within the human heart, and for the gospel which hath brought life and immortality to light. Receive our thanksgiving, reveal Thy presence, and send into our hearts the Spirit of the Risen Christ. Amen.

WILLIAM E. ORCHARD

Easter

Father God, today we give a special thanks for our mothers. They gave so much of themselves that we might be who we are today. They loved us and guided us from infancy to adulthood. May they receive this blessing with full appreciation for all they mean to us. Amen.

BOB AND EMILIE BARNES

Mother's Day

I mean her well so earnestly,
Unchanged in changing mood;
My life would go without a sigh
To bring her something good.

George MacDonald

Almighty God, our heavenly Father, in whose hands are the living and the dead; we give Thee thanks for all those Thy servants who have laid down their lives in the service of our country. Grant to them Thy mercy and the light of Thy presence, that the good work which Thou hast begun in them may be perfected; through Jesus Christ our Lord. Amen.

THE BOOK OF COMMON WORSHIP

Father God, today we give a special thanks for our fathers. They have contributed so much in developing us into who we are today. The memories are so vivid in our minds. May they always know of our love for them; they mean so much to us this day. Thank You for giving us fathers who loved and guided our growth into maturity. Amen.

Bob and Emilie Barnes

Father God, as You gave Adam the responsibility to labor in the Garden of Eden, we ask You to direct each of our labors around this table. Our country was built upon hard work. We ask that You give us a renewal about our jobs and that our excellence in labor is reflective of our love for You as our God. May You continue to be with us in our toils. Amen.

BOB AND EMILIE BARNES

O Lord, our God, who through Thy Son Jesus Christ
hast consecrated labor to the welfare of mankind,
prosper, we pray Thee, the industries of this
land; bless all those who are engaged therein; shield
them in their dangers and temptations,
and grant that, receiving the due fruits of their labors,
they may praise Thee by living according to
Thy will; through the same
Jesus Christ our Lord. Amen.

Acts of Devotion

Lord, be with us on this day of Thanksgiving,

Help us make the most of this life we are living.

As we are about to partake of this bountiful meal

Let us not forget the needy and the hunger they feel.

Help us to show compassion in all that we do,

And for all our many blessings we say thank You. Amen.

HELEN LATHAM

Let all of us…give thanks to God

and prayerful contemplation to those eternal truths

and universal principles of Holy Scripture

which have inspired such measure

of true greatness as this nation has achieved.

Dwight D. Eisenhower, Thanksgiving Proclamation, 1956

Thanksgiving

Let us…give thanks to God
for His graciousness and
generosity to us—pledge
to Him our everlasting devotion—
beseech His divine guidance
and the wisdom and
strength to recognize and
follow that guidance.

LYNDON B. JOHNSON,
THANKSGIVING PROCLAMATION, 1964

Let us observe this day
with reverence and with
prayer that will rekindle in us
the will and show us
the way not only to preserve
our blessings, but also to
extend them to the four
corners of the earth.

JOHN F. KENNEDY,
THANKSGIVING PROCLAMATION, 1961

Almighty God and Father of light,
a child is born for us and a son is given to us.
Your eternal Word leaped down from heaven
in the silent watches of the night,
and now your Church is filled with wonder
at the nearness of our God.

Open your heart to receive His life
and increase our vision with the rising of dawn,
that our life may be filled with His glory
    and peace,
who lives and reigns for ever and ever. Amen.

A CHRISTIAN PRAYER

Almighty and everlasting God, who art
the Brightness of faithful souls and the
Desire of all nations; so fill the world with Thy
glory and show Thyself by the radiance of
Thy light that all the peoples of the earth
may be subject unto Thee; through Jesus Christ
our Lord. Amen.

PRAYERS FOR THE CHRISTIAN YEAR

Advent

Christmas Eve

O God who hast made this
most hallowed night
resplendent with the glory of
the true Light;
grant that we who have
known the mysteries of that
Light on earth,
may enter into the
fullness of His joys in heaven.

Christmas Midnight, Western Rite

O gentle baby Jesus,
In the manger lying,
Dost Thou know that round Thy head
The children's prayers are flying?
Come in the blessed season
Everyone is keeping;
All the children north and south
Pray to Jesus, sleeping.

Christmas

O gentle baby Jesus,
In the manger lying,
Dost Thou know that round Thy head
The children's prayers are flying?

"Oh Jesus, let me follow
Thy way of selfless giving;
Take my hand to lead me on
Thy road of gentle living."

O gentle baby Jesus,
In the manger lying,
Dost Thou know that round Thy head
The children's prayers are flying?

Author Unknown

O Father, who hast declared Thy love to men by the birth of the Holy Child at Bethlehem; help us to welcome Him with gladness and to make room for Him in our common days; so that we may live at peace with one another and in good will with all Thy family; through the same Thy Son, Jesus Christ our Lord. Amen.

PRAYERS FOR THE CHRISTIAN YEAR

Father God, may the spirit of giving,
Go on through the year,
Bringing love, laughter,
Hope, and good cheer.
Gifts wrapped with charity,
Joy, peace, and grace,
Ribboned with happiness,
A tender embrace.

NORMA WOODBRIDGE

Christmas

New Year's Eve

*Father God, tonight we celebrate
the ending of another year.
May we have used it to Your glory.
As we reflect back over the events of the year,
we thank You for all the guidance and
strength each day. Without Your support
the past would not have the same purpose.
Please renew our vision and strength
for what is ahead. Amen.*

Bob and Emilie Barnes

PRAYERS FROM
Other Lands

May there always be work for your hands
to do
May your purse always hold a coin or two
May the sun always shine upon your
windowpane
May a rainbow be certain to follow each rain
May the hand of a friend always be near to
you and
May God fill your heart with gladness to
cheer you. Amen.

An Irish Blessing

May the road rise to meet you,
May the wind be always at your back,
May the sun shine warm on your face,
The rain fall softly on your fields;
And until we meet again,
May God hold you in the palm of His hand.
Amen.

An Irish Blessing

Praised be Thou, O God, who dost make the day bright with Thy sunshine, and the night with the beams of heavenly fires. Listen now to my prayers; watch over me with Thy power; give me grace to pass all the days of my life blamelessly, free from sin and terror. For with Thee is mercy and plenteous redemption, O Lord, my God. Amen.

LITURGY OF THE GREEK CHURCH

O God, You fill the hungry with good things. Send Your blessing on us, as we work
   in this kitchen,
And make us ever thankful for our
   daily bread.
Grant this through Christ our Lord.
   Amen.

AN OLD BASQUE BLESSING

May God grant you always...
     A sunbeam to warm you,
A moonbeam to charm you,
     A sheltering angel
So nothing can harm you...

An Irish Prayer

When we clasp our hands in prayer, God opens His.

GERMAN PROVERB

Father God, my guardian, watch over our home from top to bottom; from one corner to the other; from east to west; from the side facing the sea; from the inside to the outside. Watch over and protect it; ward off all that may trouble our life here. Amen.

A HAWAIIAN PRAYER

Hear
my prayer,
O Lord

PSALM 86:6